LABELS of DISTINCTION
MICROBREWERY LABEL DESIGN

SPENCER DRATE AND THOMAS OLEJAR

FOREWORD BY CHARLES FINKEL · BACKWORD BY DANIEL BRADFORD

GinGko
PRESS

ACKNOWLEDGEMENTS

The authors would like to acknowledge the following people for the successful creation of this book: Gerald McConnell and the people of Madison Square Press for their vision and patience; Charles Finkel and Daniel Bradford of *All About Beer* magazine for thier contribution of labels; and the designers from each region for their invaluable commentaries and insight. Thomas would like to thank Bob and Mercedes for their constancy, and everyone who has shared a good pint and story, especially Eric, Skippy, Jeff R., Bill, Big, Dutch, Dave F. and Brook. Spencer would like to thank: Jütka Salavetz, Justin and Ariel, all the breweries that contributed to the book, all of the designers that "paint" the labels, and Michael A. Klotz of Klotz Graphix for unifying the vision.

Labels of Distinction
Copyright 1998 by Spencer Drate

ISBN 3-927258-64-4
Library of Congress Catalog Card Number 97-075831

Book and Cover design by Spencer Drate and Michael A. Klotz
Photographs supplied by Anchor Brewing Co. & JVNW, Inc.

Distributed throughout the world by:
Hearst Books International 1350 Avenue of the Americas New York, New York 10019

Published by:
Ginko Press, Inc. 5768 Paradise Dr., Suite J, Corte Madera, Ca 94925 USA
Fax: (415) 924-9608, Phone (415) 924-9615 email: ginko@linex.com

Printed in Hong Kong

This book is dedicated to those
who pursue their muse with disregard to ambition,
who proceed with great abandon into the judgement of society,
who venture out without a martyr's pride,
and who lead the way for the rest of us.

TABLE OF CONTENTS

FOREWORD

Quite often, after someone finds out that I design beer labels, they let me in on a little secret of theirs: "Labels significantly influence their purchases." They then typically offer an example of a beer they are proud to know about, but which they presume is somewhat obscure. Not wanting to appear unappreciative of their confidence and advice, I usually just smile and thank them for their insight.

Of course labels influence our beer purchases! In one concise document, more or less the brew's birth certificate, we are able to learn its name, type, taste, recipe, usage, origin, history, strength, content and even medals and awards it has garnered. If we are lucky, the designer reaches out to our senses with handsome illustrations, harmonious colors and titillating type. Slogans can elevate the text from prose to poetry. Although the physical document is called a label, what we are really talking about is the image of the product. Simply said, when it comes to microbrews, what that image promises makes people purchase one brand over another.

The successful selling of beer is as much about marketing as it is about brewing. It has often been said: "It is harder to sell good beer than it is to make it." Some beer labels are good, others are classic, but in the final analysis, it is the suds that must deliver that which the label promises. This is particularly true of microbrewed beers—those without big advertising budgets. Good beers sometimes have awful labels. Occasionally a blockbuster label will adorn a poor beer but those are the exceptions. Attention to detail separates the marvelous from the mainstream. Good marketers pay as much attention to their type choices as they do their malt and hops. Consumers know, if only intuitively, that a product with a good package often delivers.

A BRIEF HISTORY OF MICROBREW LABELS:

Although the term "microbrew" is relatively new, having its origin on the west coast of the U.S. in the 1980s, the concept of craft beer is over 9,000 years old. Common or factory brewers, those that deliver to more than just their own pubs, developed around the time that printing became widespread. Labels were first used on wooden kegs, and as machine-made glass became available, on bottled products. In the 19th century, label design developed as an art form alongside technical developments in printing. Since most labels were applied by hand, oval and die-cut shapes were common. Most type was hand drawn with ornate outlines and shadows. Before the advent of mass-market media such as radio and TV, labels and point-of-sales advertising were the only opportunity brewers had to advertise their products.

It was prohibition, from 1919 until 1933, that put America's 2,700 brewers out of business. With repeal came the advent of mass-market advertising and with it, ersatz beer. The relatively few brewers who were able to withstand the curse of prohibition reinvented beer, making it from barley malt with the addition of corn and rice filler, euphemistically called adjunct. In the same way, bakers, dairies and other food producers learned to use high percentages of filler, additives and preservatives to produce tasteless white bread, "cheese food" and non-dairy "whitener." They all traded quality and authenticity for advertising dollars. Labels, like the beers they adorned, became dull and listless. They were usually small squares or rectangular shapes, typeset with "modern" stylized lettering. As consolidation continued, brewers copied one another with beers and labels of similar type.

The very term beer is a derivative of its principal ingredient, barley Hordeum vulgare. Beerlec (beerplant) was the English term for both the plant and the brew. The Bavarian purity law, the "Reingeitsgebot" of 1516 is said to be the world's earliest pure food law. It said that beer could be made only with malted (germinated) barley, hops and water. Today, any microbrewer worth his salt uses all malt along with hops as a seasoning and natural preservative, yeast to ferment the barley sugar into alcohol and natural carbonation, and pure water. One mass-market beer, by contrast, is made from 39 ingredients including many preservatives, chemicals and additives. No wonder that the term microbrew struck a cord with consumers interested in a good beer.

Craft beers have grown from a minuscule percentage of the U.S. market at the time the term microbrew was first invented, to almost 10% of the market today. In 1980, only a handful of American, English, Belgian and German all-malt beers were available to American consumers. America now boasts over 1,500 breweries and hundreds of high- quality imports are widely distributed. As the field has become more and more crowded, microbrewers here and throughout the world are discovering the importance of good label design. Surprisingly little has been presented about this colorful topic—until now.

Whether you are a professional designer or simply a beer enthusiast, celebrate the art of brewing. Pour yourself a beautifully labeled microbrew, find an easy chair, and relax with Labels of Distinction.

Cheers,

Charles Finkel,
Seattle, Washington

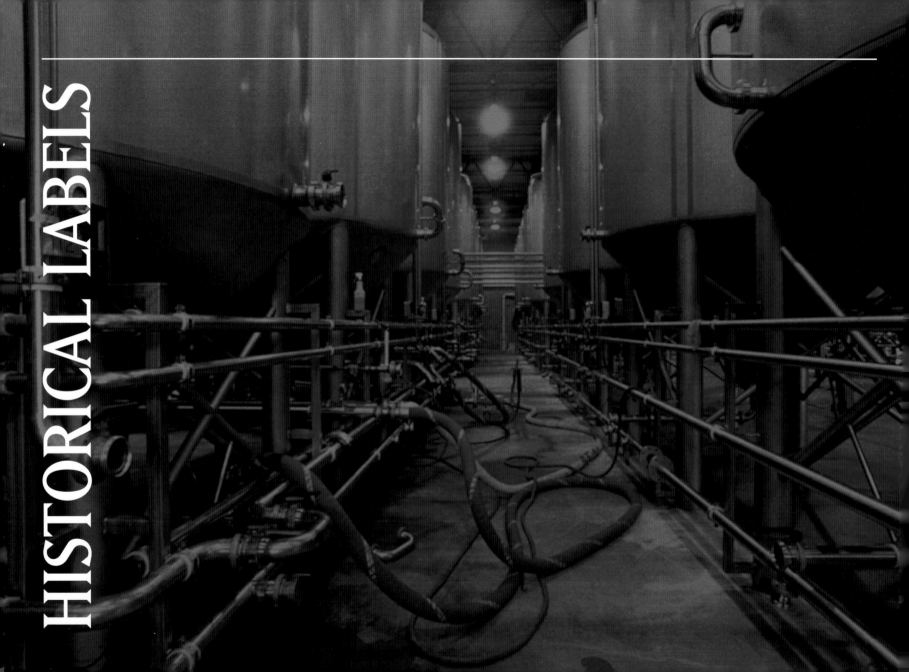

HISTORICAL LABELS

Mounted Belgian cowboys lassoing beer bottles which are labeled with the same Belgian cowboys in miniature; tiny gnomes brewing a strange malty elixir far below the earth's surface; partying merry monks; beer in chubby hands; Noah's menagerie of horses, dogs, tigers, lions, birds, goats and bears, all savoring the delight of zymotechnic alchemy and—best of all—each work of art available for the price of a bottled beer, usually a good one at that.

Label design reached its imaginative, artistic, technical and sensual climax during the late 18th and early 19th centuries. Images in color, printing techniques, illustrations and lettering had to appeal to a broad number of consumers—from those who could read, to those who could only recognize a symbol—in order for them to become repeat customers. As fantasy turned to fact, serious brands developed. To study the evolution of label design, presented here is a selection of choice specimens from this pre-mass-market-mentality era.

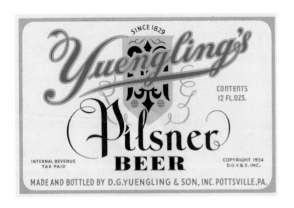

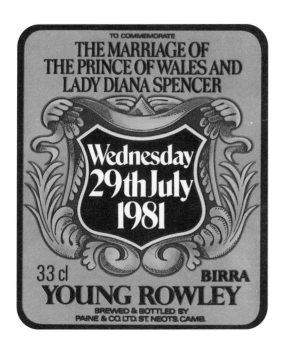

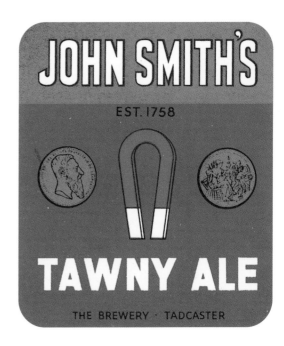

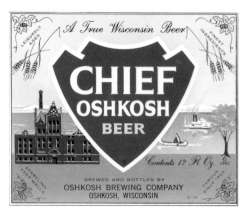

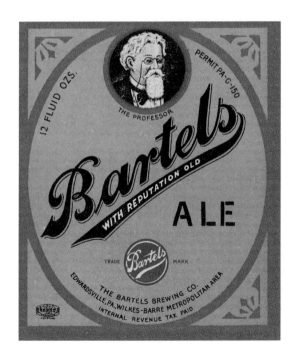

BASS & CO'S PALE ALE

THIS LABEL IS ISSUED ONLY BY BASS, RATCLIFF & GRETTON. LIMITED

TRADE MARK.

Bass & Co

B 726

BOTTLED BY
Sté C. DELEVOY,
FR. DU ROI.

BREWERS, BURTON - ON - TRENT

BOCK-BIER

BRAUEREI INTERLAKEN

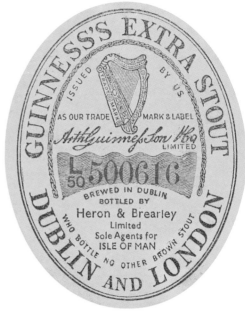

GUINNESS'S EXTRA STOUT

ISSUED — BY US

AS OUR TRADE MARK & LABEL

Arth.Guinness Son & Co
LIMITED

L 50 500616

BREWED IN DUBLIN
BOTTLED BY

Heron & Brearley
Limited
Sole Agents for
ISLE OF MAN

WHO BOTTLE NO OTHER BROWN STOUT

DUBLIN AND LONDON

4

Bayerische Staats-Brauerei-Weihenstephan

Seit 1146

Starkbier Corbinian
Dunkel

Old fashioned Lager

Since 1874

Beer

THIS BEER DOES NOT CONTAIN MORE THAN FOUR PER CENTUM OF ALCOHOL BY WEIGHT

HIVE'S BREWERY

FOR BELGIUM IS THIS LABEL ONLY ISSUED BY F.F. THIENPONT

TRADE MARK & LABEL

TRIUMPH
STOUT

BOTTLED BY

BREWERS ETICHOVE BELGIUM

E. SMITHWICK AND SONS LIMITED

SMITHWICK'S No1 ALE

Established 1710

BOTTLED BEER COMPETITION · 1937 · 1st PRIZE

Bottled by

B

ST. FRANCIS ABBEY BREWERY, KILKENNY.

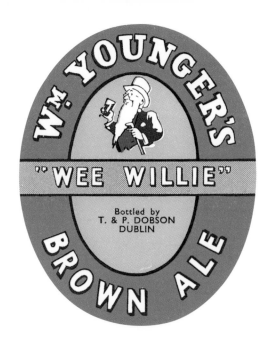

WM YOUNGER'S

"WEE WILLIE"

Bottled by
T. & P. DOBSON
DUBLIN

BROWN ALE

THIS LABEL IS ISSUED ONLY BY BASS. RATCLIFF & GRETTON LIMITED

BASS & Co's No1 BARLEY WINE

TRADE MARK

Bass & Co

A 163

BREWERS. BURTON - ON - TRENT

THIS LABEL IS ISSUED ONLY BY W. McEWAN & Co Ltd

McEWAN'S

EDINBURGH

SCOTCH ALE

BREWERS   EDINBURGH

SUPER

FINE SPÉCIALITÉ

CATÉG. SUPÉRIEURE

⅓ L.

COW-BOY

R.C.C. 5707

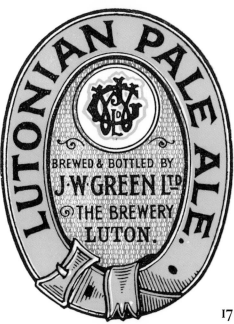

LUTONIAN PALE ALE

BREWED & BOTTLED BY

J W GREEN Ltd

THE BREWERY LUTON.

17

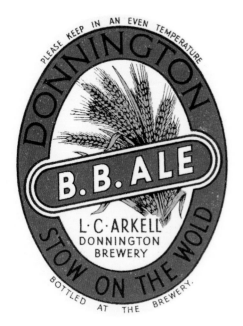

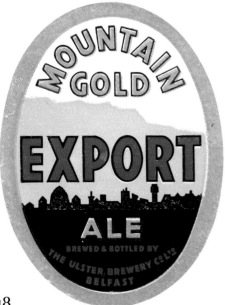

18

BRASSERIE LEMETTE
BIÈRE FINE
BERNEVILLE

LEVERANDØR TIL · DET KGL.DANSKE HOF
TUBORGS · BRYGGERIER
VARE T MÆRKE
TUBORG
Brygget siden
1875
LAGER · ØL
BRYGGET AF MALT RÅFRUGT OG HUMLE JUSTERET MED ANTIOXIDANT, SUKKERKULØR OG ANDRE TILSÆTNINGSSTOFFER

LANDSØL
LARVIKS
BRYGGERIER

EXTRA STOUT
LLB
QUALITÉ SUPÉRIEURE

BRASSERIE TIVOLI
MARQUE · DÉPOSÉE
THONY'S BEER
BIÈRE D'EXPORTATION
garantie pure et dépourvue de
tous produits chimiques
AGENT GÉNÉRAL
ANTHONY SCHNEIDER
··ANVERS··
ANVERS
MISE EN BOUTEILLES À LA BRASSERIE·

KRIEK
1/3 L
BR. RODE A-RODE-ST-GENÈSE
TEL. RODE.58.00.87·58.04.21

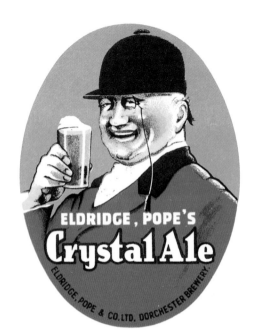

20

HANSA
BRYGGERI.
BAYERSK ØL
BERGEN

Stout extra
BRASSERIE DU CENTRE
E. François-Renaux
SELOIGNES
Téléphone 7
IMP. RAMBOUX-GALLOT-THUILLIES

AKTIESELSKAPET
Lilloe
Bok Øl
DRAMMEN
CHRISTIAN WRIEDTs BRYGGERI

BROWAR CIECHANÓW
ROK ZAŁ.
1864
ZAW. ALK. DO 25 %   PN-55A-79092
PIWO
słodowe specjalne
C
POJ. 0,5 L.   CENA Zł 2.40

SAISON DE PIPAIX
MARQUE   DÉPOSÉE
BRASSERIE
BISET-CUVELIER

DET · KONGELIG · DANSKE · HOF
Carlsberg
Pilsner
CARLSBERG · LEVERANDØR · TIL

BRASSERIE DE LA SOYE
GÉROUVILLE
DOUBLE

A/s CHR. WRIEDTS BRYGGERI &
JULEØL
MINERALVANDFABRIK

A/s P.LTZ. AASS. BRYGGERI
Imported by Merchant du Vin Corp. · Seattle, WA
Brewed and bottled by Aass Brewery, Drammen, Norway
AASS BOKK
DRAMMEN, NORWAY
12 fl. oz.   Product of Norway

LUNDETANGEN'S BRYGGERI
GRAND PRIX PARIS 1907
BERGEN 1898
KJØBENHAVN 1872
STOCKHOLM 1866
ALKOHOLFRIT
VØRTER-ØL
GULDMEDALIE   GULDMEDALIE
LANDS-
UDSTILLINGEN
SKIEN
1891
JUBILEUMS-
UDSTILLINGEN
PORSGRUND
1907
SKIEN

LEVERANDØR TIL DET KGL. DANSKE HOF
PRIMA HVIDTØL
C. WIIBROES BRYGGERI
KRONBORG BRYG
HELSINGØR

PILSNER·ØL
TRADE   MARK
MACK-ØL
A/S L. MACKS ØLBRYGGERI · TROMSØ

THE EAST

New York City is the Capital of the World. The statement is not simply some city government propaganda, as much as it is a reality. The island of Manhattan is a concrete jungle where decisions affecting the entire world are made every minute. Anything can be bought, sold, traded or seen, and those who are too weak for its biting temperament are gobbled up and spit out. But those who live in the city know that if you venture not too far outside of the city, placid landscapes and rustic villages are quite the norm. This is the makeup of most of the Eastern Seaboard. Mention of the area summons up images of urban centers such as New York, Boston, Philadelphia and Washington D.C., but the vast majority of the region retains much of its colonial charm.

The microbrewing renaissance in the East sprang forth in both the larger cities and in the rustic countryside. New York City was actually a slow market to mature. At first, specialty beer products were available only at "beer bars," but as tastes changed brewpubs began to open in many neighborhoods. One such small brewery, Chelsea Brewing Company, opened several years ago and serves as the city's sole commercial bottling facility. Spencer Drate (co-author), when commissioned to create labels for their blonde ale, was struck with the common problem of designing to capture a New York City feel. "It is so easy to be cliché and obvious, such as using the Statue of Liberty," Spencer declares in his patented New York accent. "The label had to be New York attitude and jump off the shelf at you, but at the same time be original and familiar." The result was a yellow, black and white "Checker Cab" design utilizing typeface imitating a license plate. The theme was so prevalent in the label, that the brewery decided to simply name the blonde ale "Checker Cab Blonde Ale."

Spencer, who is a creative director of his own studio and a leading CD and book package designer, quickly assimilated the New York attitude as applied to beer label design:

"This is New York, a city where a sports season ends when the New York team has been eliminated. Being on this island is a psychological trip, so you have to feed off of this egocentricity. I think that is true in certain pockets of America where the design has to be an almost "inside joke" to the native consumer. This helped the Chelsea products to get into Grand Central Station and Yankee Stadium.

"It is a remarkably natural transition coming from designing for famous Rock 'n Roll artists into beer label design. It's a relatively untamed territory that allows for a lot of freedom to be expressive, albeit on a very small canvas. The designers and the brewery owners of the last decade in America need to be given a lot of credit for eliminating the rules for design and for breaking down all of the preconceived notions of what a beer label should look like. Now, you have this wonderful practice (whether consciously undertaken or not) of making labels look like the beer tastes. It's absolutely wild and refreshing."

Each of the great cities of the East—New York, Boston, Baltimore, Philadelphia and Washington D.C.—have developed their own maturing beer cultures. Brewpubs and small microbreweries have made a comeback, finally recovering from what Prohibition and World War II did to eliminate them from existence. Moreover, these small breweries are assimilating aspects of each city's personality into their labeling. These cities, being the oldest in America, have more to draw upon than other areas of the country, and designers will smartly capitalize on the proud history of each place.

Whether it's Charm City, Bean Town, the Big Apple or the rural countryside, it is in the East where the country begins, and where the designers have to beware the traps of mediocrity. Beer label design, here, has survived such traps.

VERMONT

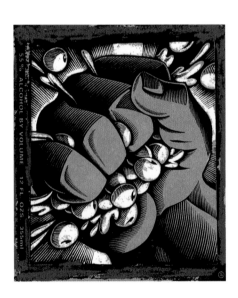

ATLANTIC CITY

NEW JERSEY

CASCO BAY

MAINE

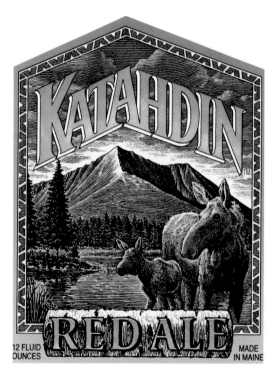

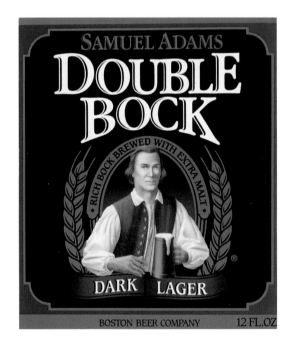

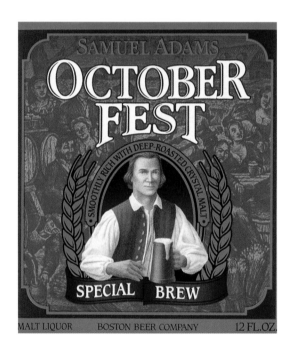

BREWERY HILL BREWING CO., INC.

PENNSYLVANIA

BROOKLYN BREWERY

NEW YORK

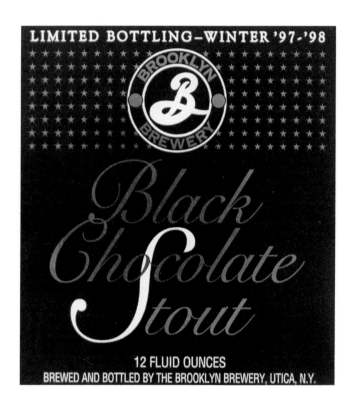

BROOKLYN BREWERY

NEW YORK

Chelsea Brewing Co.

NEW YORK

Elk Mountain

NEW HAMPSHIRE

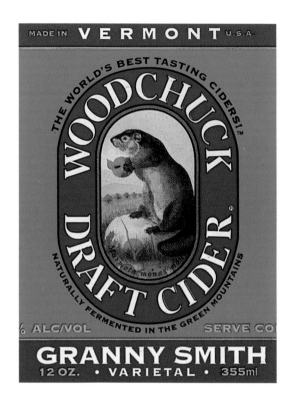

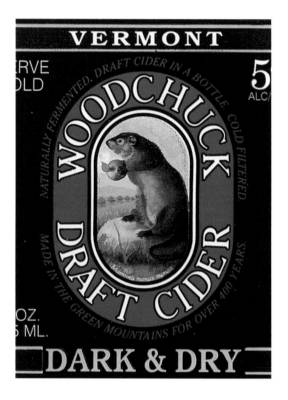

LATROBE BREWING CO.

PENNSYLVANIA

MAGIC HAT BREWING COMPANY

VERMONT

VERMONT

Mass. Bay Brewing Co., Inc.

MASSACHUSETTS

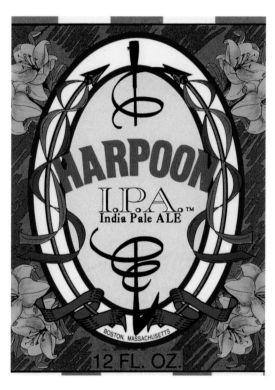

Mass. Bay Brewing Co., Inc.

MASSACHUSETTS

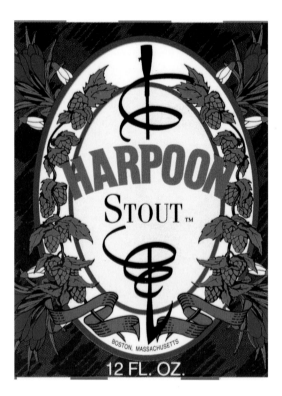

36

MYSTIC SEAPORT

MAINE

OLD DOMINION BREWING CO.

PENNSYLVANIA

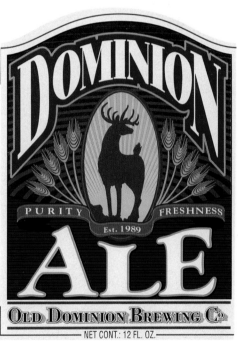

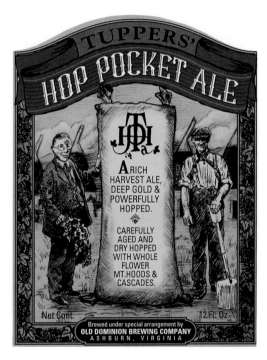

OTTER CREEK BREWING, INC.

VERMONT

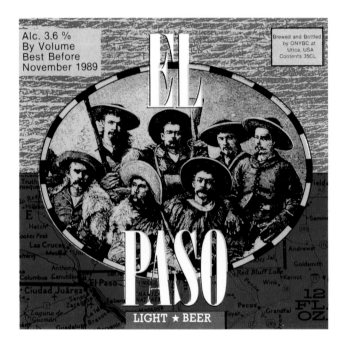

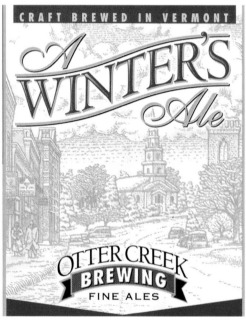

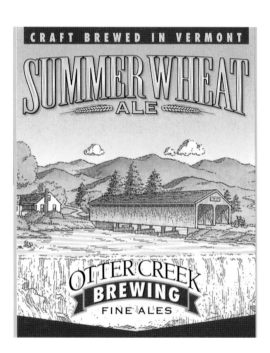

ROCKFORD BREWING CO.

DELAWARE

STEGMAIER BREWING CO.

PENNSYLVANIA

WAINWRIGHT

PENNSYLVANIA

39

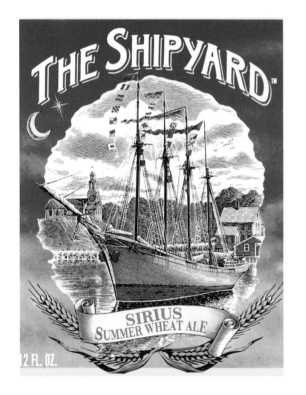

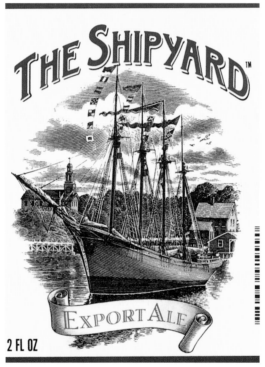

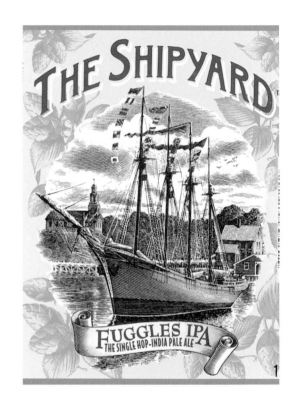

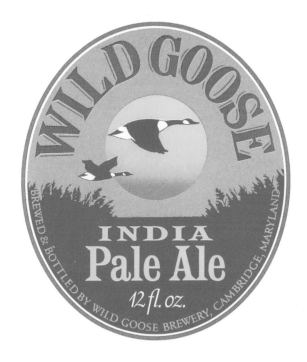

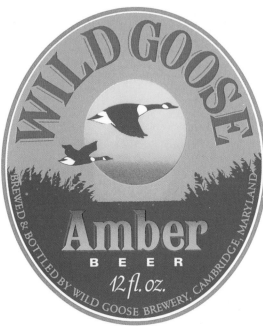

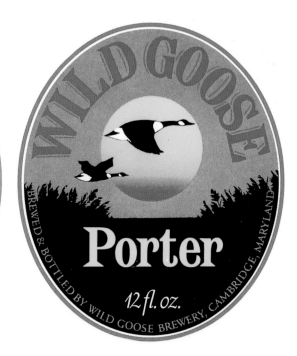

THE SOUTH

The genuine American arts—jazz and the blues—originated in the South and evolved metaphorically up Highway 61 through St. Louis and Chicago and then on to the rest of the country. Unfortunately, traffic going the other way seems to be a bitch. In regards to the recapturing of craft brewing in America, this is certainly true. The actual legal feasibility of small-scale brewing, particularly brewpubs, has just come to pass in many Southern states.

The Southern states, particularly those of the Mississippi Valley, contain a captivating and often overlooked facet of American culture. Anyone who would dare offer the statement that the South is backward has never experienced the deep soulful undertones of Memphis blues, the agrarian charm of a Nashville country ballad, or the seductiveness of New Orleans Jazz.

What does exist in the South is a definite appreciation and mastery of the celebration. In a land that clings to the axiom: "Laissez les bons temps rouler" (let the good times roll), it seems a foregone conclusion that microbreweries will spring forth and facilitate the consumer demand. A perfect example of Southern imagery and this seemingly perfect opportunity for craft brewing is the Mardi Gras! This festival, most prominent in New Orleans, takes place on Fat Tuesday, the day before Lent begins. The relationship between Lent and beer is centuries old, and in the New Orleans setting you have a marriage made in heaven.

If the microbrewing revolution is truly a revolution then the Dixie Brewing Company is the feisty, tenacious squadron that won't be defeated, even though it is deep behind enemy lines. The eerie, dream-like packaging of their products symbolizes the rest of the country's fascination with the Southern mystique. Using "Voodoo" in the product description only contributes to our cryptic assessment of the brewery. Another Southern brewery, the Yellow Rose Brewery, took a different approach. Glen Fritz, the label designer and head brewer at the Yellow Rose Brewery, is keenly aware of the "nostalgic" elements of Southern influence:

"What other area of America has the ghosts of Conquistadors, Indians, statesmen and soldiers haunting its modern streets? Framed by old ranch names echoing from rolling green mountains to rocky, arid hills, to lush and expansive flatlands, breweries in the South are fortunate to be located in a rich environment, conducive to creativity and nostalgic imagery... Who needs an imagination to design beer labels in surroundings such as these?

"Yes, the label graphics need to be distinctive enough to woo a potential customer unfamiliar with the product amid a confusing plethora of stimuli in the typical beer section. The poor bottle needs to be prepared to bare its heart and soul if it is to have a chance to plead its case to a momentary glance from prodding eyes. Any feat of success is accomplished in the heart and not the mind—both in the heart of the designer poured into his design, and the heart and emotion of the buyer. (Statistically, the emotional reaction accounts for over 85% of initial buying decisions. People then tend to seek facts to justify to their rational side that the initial inclination was good judgement!)"

From the Carolinas to Texas, Southern microbreweries are beginning to display their products with imagery from the region. This is a place where citizens remember the past, but are aware of their surroundings. Blooming magnolias, Spanish moss, cowboys and Indians, Johnny Cash and the Southern bell—absolutely American and a designer's dream of symbols to draw from.

DIXIE BREWING CO.

LOUISIANA

RIKENJAK'S BREWERY

LOUISIANA

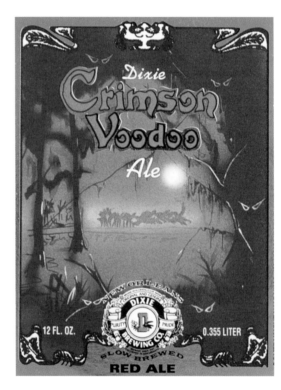

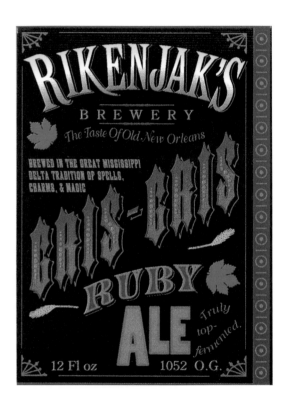

SAINT ARNOLD

TEXAS

WEEPING RADISH

NORTH CAROLINA

WILDHORSE SALOON

TENNESSEE

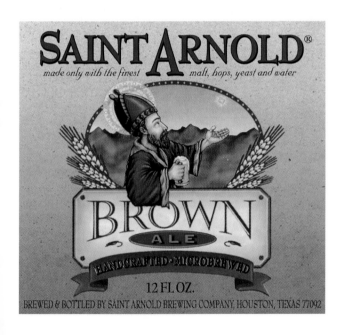

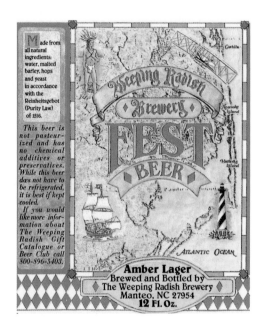

WILLIAMSVILLE BREWERY

FLORIDA

YELLOW ROSE BREWING CO.

TEXAS

46

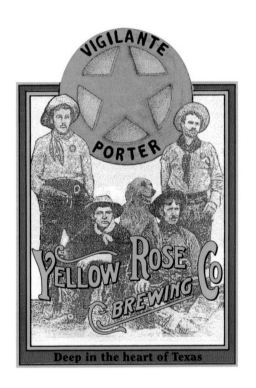

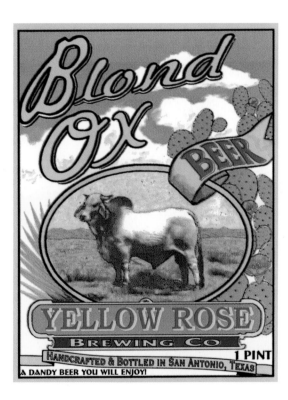

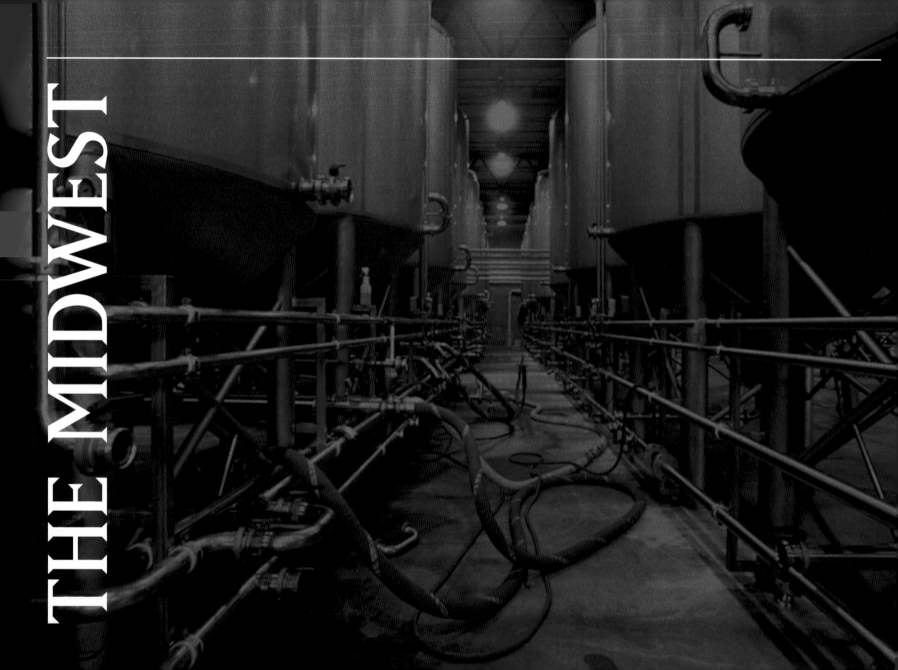

THE MIDWEST

Expansive farms, colossal factories, college football games, apple pies and Mom—are all elements that are not just American cliché but are the make up of America's heartland. This area retains all of the sense of community of America's European ancestors. The Midwestern portion of America produces more beer than anywhere else in the world, and in line with agriculture and manufacturing, the products are generally intended for the masses.

While experimentation and a sense of adventure is left to the "crazies" out in California or New York City, the Midwestern approach is more of a faith in the tried and true; riding the steady course. Cars need to be roomy, but not too "girly" like those European "jobby's," but not too small like those Japanese toy cars. Food? Make it hearty—meat and potatoes—and maybe some Great Lakes perch on a special day. Talk comes straight from the hip; E.B. White would be proud of the fact that useless words are never spoken. The beer consumed here has traditionally been an interpretation of the Bavarian styles, due to the massive immigration of Central Europeans years ago. Names like Stroh, Schlitz and Pabst proliferated the grocery store shelves for years, and Midwesterners, as always, felt comfortable with the consistency.

The microbrewing revolution, like many subtle changes in the American culture, emerged slowly amongst the dominating mainstay beer products. While drinking six-dollar coffees at pretentious coffeehouses became popular in only a few large Midwestern cities, small brewing was accepted as an honest and honorable endeavor.

The first invasion of new brewery products revealed a different style of packaging. One can almost picture the image of the new products adorning the back bar: the Bud Light, Miller Light, Stroh's, Labatt Blue, and then sitting there like the new kid in grade school, a Samuel Adams or Pete's product. New style labels with an actual picture on the front, old-style type, dark colors, not available in a can—what's the deal with these new guys?

More micros would follow, and the consumer market would have to accept the product. Packaging design in America's heartland has an almost singular purpose: to make the consumer feel comfortable with the product. No major intrusion or artistic breakthrough is necessary on the labels; earth tones and waves of grain work best. What causes this unusual acceptance of simple and pleasant packaging? Midwesterners are unencumbered by the pretensions of public ritual. In Manhattan or LA the ordering of a drink at a bar, tavern or restaurant needs to be carefully calculated in order to invoke the proper effect. "What's that fancy-looking concoction that he's drinking?" or "Wow, that's an unusual-looking beer—they must know something!" are the desired effects. Midwesterners are more often than not exhausted after the daily grind and want a familiar beer to comfort them.

Now that Midwesterners have ceased to view microbreweries as an unwanted disruption to their routine lifestyles and have learned, rather, to accept and incorporate this "revolution" as part of their culture, the Midwestern beer culture has become a natural mixture of the generic and the distinct. Bell's Amber Ale sits peacefully accepted next to the old-standard Stroh's and Miller Lite.

Randy Mosher, the region's premier label designer, describes this harmonious relationship in his outlook when designing labels in the Midwest: "... Soothe them with 'Don't I seem familiar? I'm the beer you've been waiting for all this time.' You're looking for some kind of instant relationship right there at the cooler door, built by tagging onto people's vision of how the world is. It's horribly unscientific, and you don't always get there. Clients have good or bad instincts, and without deep feelings about who they want to sell to and why, it's easy to come up with pedestrian work that has all the items ticked off the checklist, but just doesn't excite anybody. I try to use as a yardstick: "Would this idea ever have come out of a cubicle?" and chuck the ones that would. I think it's our only defense as small players in a huge market, to do crazy stuff that no big company in its right mind would ever consider. And of course, that keeps changing, because they keep copying what we're doing."

AUGUST SCHELL BREWING CO.

MINNESOTA

BARLEY BOYS BREWERY

NEBRASKA

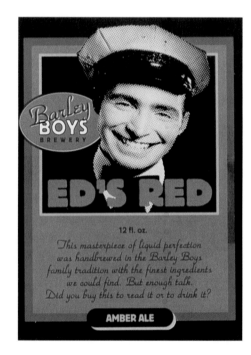

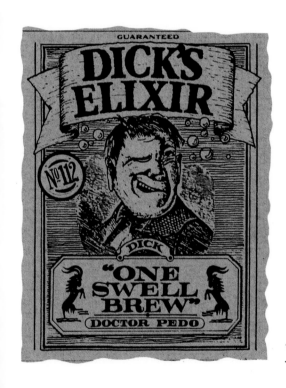

DEVIL MOUNTAIN BREWING COMPANY

OHIO

GOOSE ISLAND

ILLINOIS

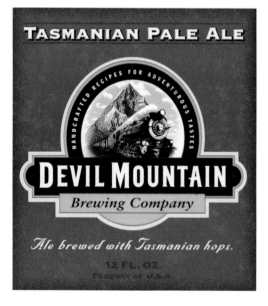

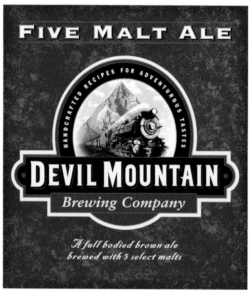

Green Bay Brewing Co.

WISCONSIN

Indianapolis Brewing Co.

INDIANA

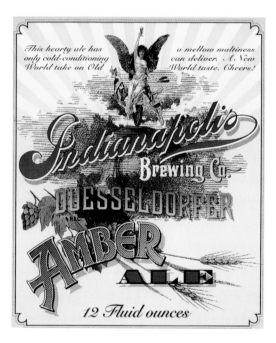

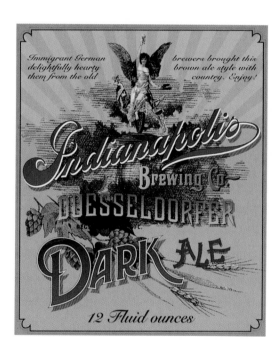

INDIANAPOLIS BREWING CO.

INDIANA

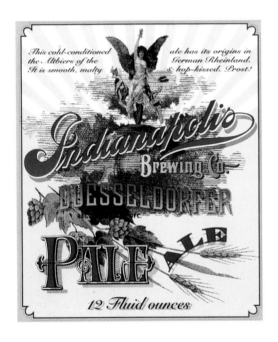

Kalamazoo Brewery

MICHIGAN

Lakefront Brewery, Inc.

WISCONSIN

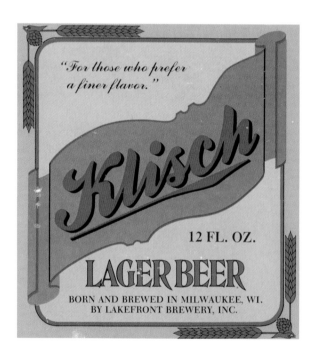

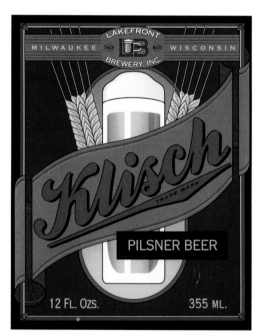

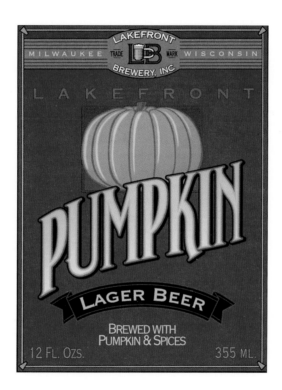

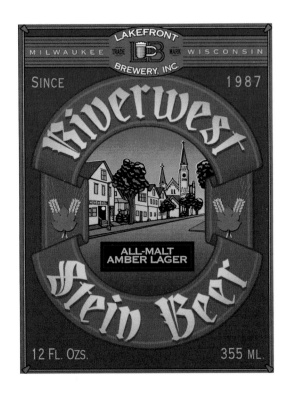

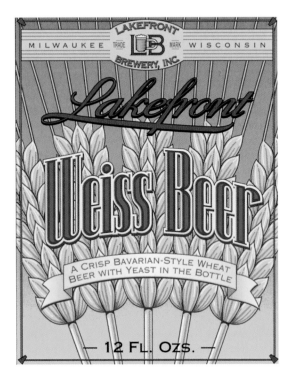

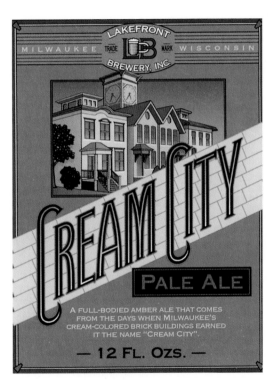

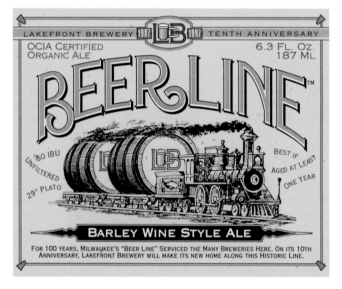

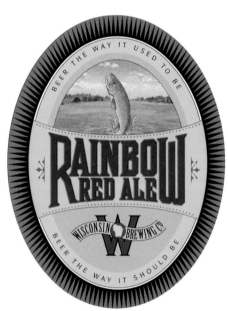

RED RIVER VALLEY BREWING CO.

MINNESOTA

ST. CROIX BREWING CO.

MINNESOTA

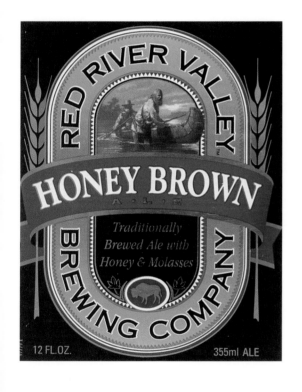

Stone City

IOWA

Tunner's Guild Brewing Co.

IOWA

THE WEST

When one ponders the phenomenal surge of the "grunge" music scene in the early 1990s the question often comes up: "How did this happen?" The blaring, incessant pounding of indecipherable lyrics haphazardly fused with a seemingly more indecipherable musical accompaniment seemed to be an unlikely voice for a generation raised in the conservative 1980s. However, in this corner of the world, they were tired of a music culture that was terminally mediocre, and the grunge movement broke through and set the tone for what would become the "alternative" music movement.

What emerged with the music movement was definitively of the West, specifically the Pacific Northwest, an area of America reminiscent of fearless trailblazers and undaunted pioneers. It was with similar bravado, albeit carried out in a more subtle fashion, that the craft brewing scene emerged from out of the West. For years, stretching back to Prohibition and World War II, the national brewing scene had been dominated by a small group (decade by decade growing smaller) of huge brewing corporations. Through the belly of this century, an overblown "Americanism" allowed for this, but factors such as increased travel abroad by Americans, home brewing, and more lenient state laws sowed a fertile ground for a craft-brewing revolution.

Seattle, known as the Emerald City, has become synonymous with quality in America. What has led to Seattle's national prominence is the city's openness to new products and ideas. The quality of the "grunge" music lay in its rage against the mainstream. The proliferation of quality beer in the area came about in a similar way, being produced by local companies who were contrasting the nation's mediocre beer culture. One of the first "pioneers" to bring quality beer to the area was beer importer, label designer, and microbrewery owner Charles Finkel (an invaluable contributor to this book). Mr. Finkel's company, Merchant du Vin, helped pave the way in the region, as well as the country, by importing some of the finest beer products from Europe. Moreover, he contributed significantly to many of these foreign brewers' label designs, and then, appropriately, to his own microbrewery in Seattle– the Pike Brewery:

"My goal in designing them was to give a naïve but serious art deco look in keeping with the nature of Seattle's Pike Market, a food lover's paradise. In creating the labels, I put on the hat of a 1930s brewery owner with a knack for stencil design. While certain elements reflect traditional European beer package design, including the obvious pride in the place where they were brewed, they needed to be All-American. I wanted them to say "Seattle" in big letters, figuratively speaking. Civic pride, in beer as in sports, is especially important, especially when only a limited advertising budget is available. A certain civic pride is reflected in the selection of Pike both on and off premise. I also wanted each label to reflect its presence as a member of a brewing family so that people who tried one and liked it, would try other styles. I did not want generic labels which could have come from anyplace."

The brewing culture that has developed in the Pacific Northwest is now quite mature as compared to much of the nation, and is remarkably diverse—almost idiosyncratic. This fact can be easily demonstrated in the viewpoints of another of the region's premier designers, Tim Girvin. Mr. Girvin takes a different approach to label design—one that clearly shows that he has a developed sense of purpose:

"The most significant issues that should be considered have to do with shelf presence. Bear in mind the significant amount of products within the beer industry, whether from large breweries or smaller microbreweries—there are so many varying labels, brand identities, typographics and colorations. The key is for supermarket shelf sets to create packaging treatments which are distinct to their individual branding system, offer consistent and cohesive messages that emanate from the center of these brands, and provide an ownable set of coloration, label structure, and brand identity management that creates an impactful presence on the shelf...."

Even now, as the smoke is clearing on the rapid expansion of craft brewing in America, trends are emanating from the West. If craft brewing identity continues to be driven by designers such as Mr. Finkel and Mr. Girvin, elegant sentimentality and market savvy will insure future success.

ALASKA

COLORADO

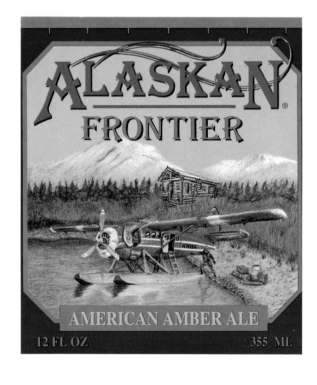

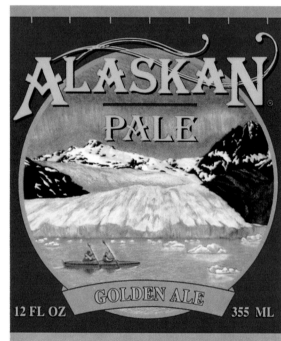

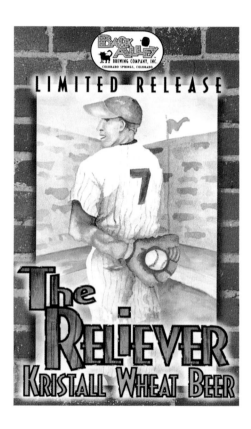

BROADWAY BREWING, L.L.C.

COLORADO

DESCHUTES BREWERY

OREGON

FULL SAIL BREWING CO.

OREGON

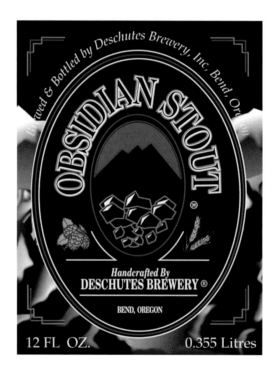

69

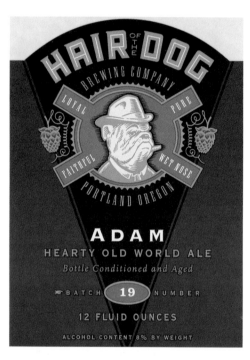

HART BREWING, INC.

WASHINGTON

Pyramid Pale Ale is a highly hopped, mahogany colored brew, balanced by an assertive malt character providing a clean, dry finish to the palate.

HART BREWING, INC.

SEATTLE•KALAMA, WA

Keep Refrigerated

Please Recycle

PYRAMID PALE ALE

12 FL. OZ. (355 ML.)

Please Recycle

Keep Refrigerated

First brewed in 1985, award winning Wheaten® Ale was the first draft wheat beer made in the United States since prohibition.

HART BREWING, INC.

Kalama, WA

PYRAMID WHEATEN ALE

12 FL. OZ.

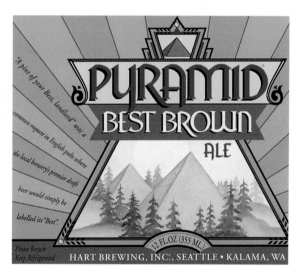

"A pint of your Best, landlord" was a common request in English pubs where the local brewery's premier draft beer would simply be labelled its "Best".

Please Recycle

Keep Refrigerated

PYRAMID BEST BROWN ALE

12 FL. OZ (355 ML.)

HART BREWING, INC., SEATTLE • KALAMA, WA

HART BREWING, INC.

WASHINGTON

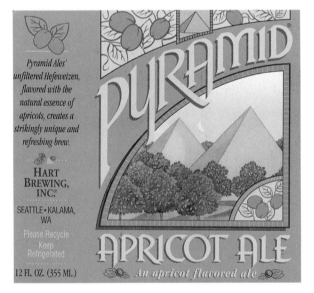

Pyramid Ales'
unfiltered Hefeweizen,
flavored with the
natural essence of
apricots, creates a
strikingly unique and
refreshing brew.

HART
BREWING,
INC.®

SEATTLE · KALAMA,
WA

Please Recycle
Keep
Refrigerated

12 FL. OZ. (355 ML.)

PYRAMID®

APRICOT ALE
An apricot flavored ale

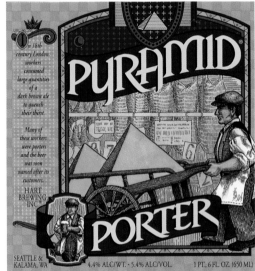

In 18th
century London,
workers
consumed
large quantities
of a
dark brown ale
to quench
their thirst.

Many of
these workers
were porters
and the beer
was soon
named after its
customers.

HART
BREWING,
INC.

SEATTLE &
KALAMA, WA

4.4% ALC/WT. · 5.4% ALC/VOL.

PYRAMID®

PORTER

1 PT., 6 FL. OZ. (650 ML.)

< German >
Hefeweizen:
"Wheat-brewed
ale with yeast"

How to Pour:
Gently
agitate bottle
before pouring

HART
BREWING,
INC.®

SEATTLE
·
KALAMA,
WA

Please Recycle

PYRAMID®

HEFEWEIZEN
ALE

1 PT., 6 FL. OZ.
(650 ML.)

Keep Refrigerated

72

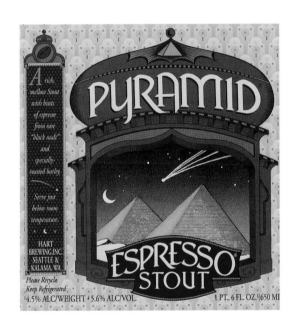

HIGH COUNTRY

COLORADO

JET CITY

WASHINGTON

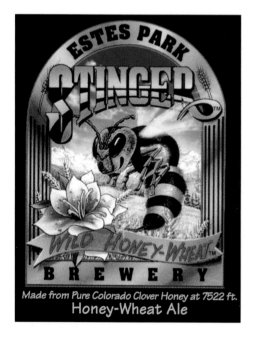

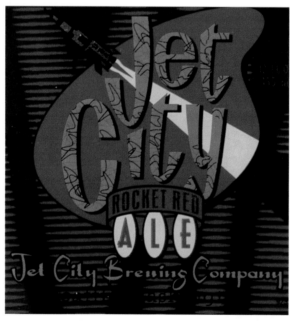

MICRO 99

OREGON

MIDNIGHT SUN BREWING COMPANY

ALASKA

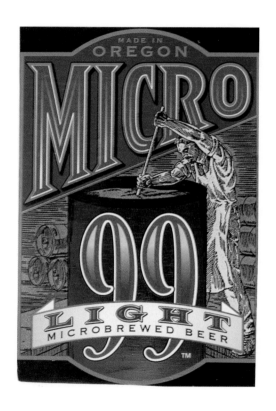

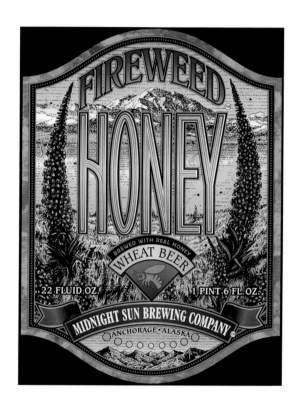

ALASKA

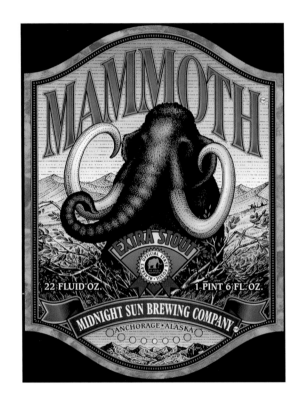

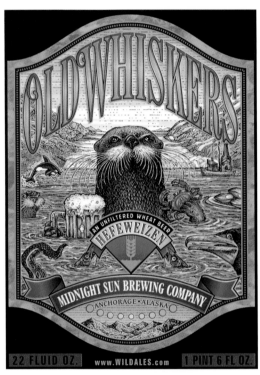

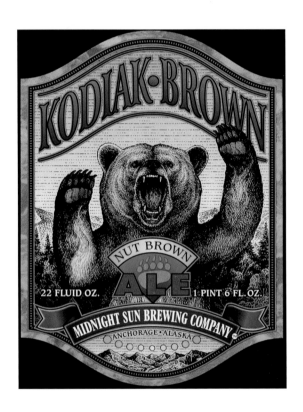

Pike Brewing Co.

ROCKIES BREWING CO.

COLORADO

ROGUE ALES

OREGON

SELKIRK CIDER CO., INC.

IDAHO

SONORA BREWING COMPANY

ARIZONA

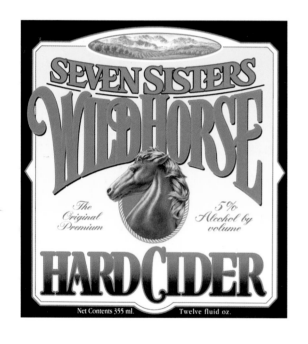

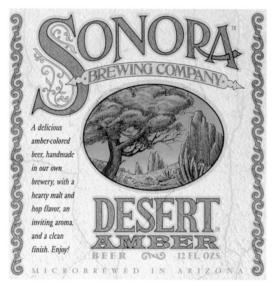

Spanish Peaks

MONTANA

The Redhook Ale Brewery

WASHINGTON

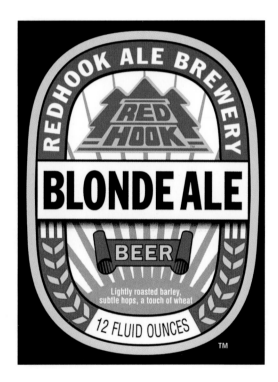

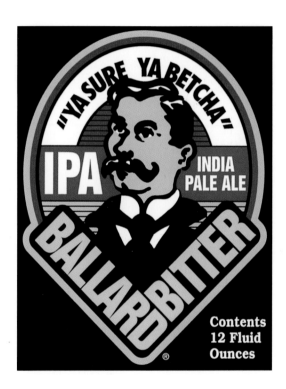

Rio Grande Brewing Co.

NEW MEXICO

Thomas Kemper Brewing Company

WASHINGTON

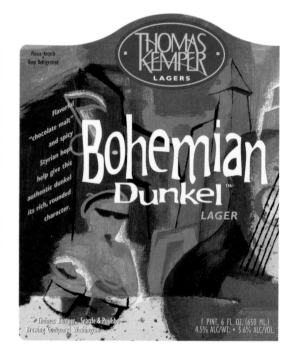

THOMAS KEMPER
LAGERS ®

Oktoberfest
Lager

A robust, copper-colored brew with a sweet, nutty, malty character and a spicy finish from Hersbrucker hops.

THOMAS KEMPER BREWING COMPANY

◆ SEATTLE & POULSBO, WASHINGTON

1 PINT, 6 FL. OZ. (650 ML.)
4.5% ALC/WT. • 5.6% ALC/VOL.

THOMAS KEMPER
LAGERS ®

Highly-roasted "black" malt and aromatic Styrian hops give this smooth winter brew its robust, bittersweet character.

WinterBräu
LAGER

THOMAS KEMPER BREWING COMPANY

SEATTLE ~ POULSBO WASHINGTON

1 PINT 6 FL. OZ. (650 ML.)
4.9% ALC/WT. • 6.1% ALC/VOL.

THOMAS KEMPER
LAGERS ®

Amber
LAGER

THOMAS KEMPER BREWING COMPANY

SEATTLE & POULSBO WASHINGTON

1 PINT 6 FL. OZ. (650 ML.)
4% ALC/WT. • 5% ALC/VOL.

THOMAS KEMPER BREWING COMPANY

WASHINGTON

Helles
(German,"light")
lager is brewed
with Oregon
blueberries and
a unique yeast
known for its
fruitiness and
aromatic qualities.
The refreshing
result is a light
bodied lager with
a subtle hint of
blueberry in
the nose and
on the palate.

Kemper
Brewing Company
Poulsbo, WA

Please Recycle
Keep Refrigerated

HELLES
BLUEBERRY LAGER
LAGER
BREWED WITH
BLUEBERRIES

1 PT., 6 FL.OZ.
(650 ML)

Please Recycle
Keep Refrigerated

The first
lagers were
brewed in
the 1830's
by Spaten
in Munich.
Like Thomas
Kemper's
Dark, these
early lagers
were dark
brown and
became
known as the
"Munchener"
style.

Thomas Kemper
Brewing Company

Seattle • Poulsbo
Washington

DARK
LAGER

1 PINT 6 FL. OZ. (650 ML.)
4.5% ALC/WT. • 5.6% ALC/VOL.

refreshing,
cloudy brew
with a malty-
sweet flavor
and a soft,
yeasty aroma.

THOMAS KEMPER
BREWING COMPANY
SEATTLE & POULSBO, WA

Hefeweizen

Unfiltered Wheat Beer
12 FL. OZ. (355 ML.)

WIDMER BROTHERS

OREGON

WILLIAMETTE VALLEY

OREGON

WILLIAMETTE VALLEY

OREGON

WYNKOOP BREWING COMPANY

COLORADO

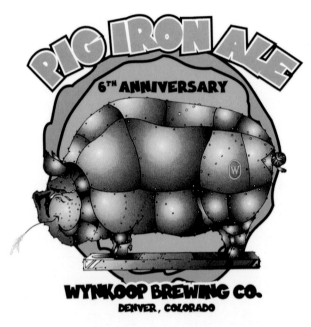

Yakima Brewing & Malting Co.

WASHINGTON

CALIFORNIA

California by itself has one of the largest economies in the world. Add to that the fact that it is tied to the remainder of the United States and you have a society that has the freedom and the means to accomplish anything. From software to wine to hockey players, California creates or assimilates whatever is the superlative in an industry.

The dawning of the microbrewing renaissance found much of its initial momentum in California. When small-scale brewing reemerged in America twenty years ago, it was in California. America's two most celebrated breweries (Anchor and Sierra Nevada) are in California. The one true American beer style (Steam Beer) was contrived and is produced only in California. Not unusual then, is the fact that some of the most extraordinary and classic beer labels come from the Golden State.

A considerable impetus for the early success of small, craft breweries in America was the emergence of the wine industry in Northern California. Napa and Sonoma counties matured as world-class wine regions and can now confidently boast about producing some of the best wines on earth. When small breweries began to appear in the same region, consumers were sympathetic of the emergent American products, and were willing to give them a chance based on the success of the area's wine products. In the nearest metropolis, San Francisco, small-scale breweries would experience enormous success that continues to this day.

Two breweries, Anchor and Sierra Nevada, best exemplify the potential of small-scale brewing. Anchor, with its hallmark anchor adorning its trademarked Steam beer style, portrays their beer in a classic, clear and elegant manner. The anchor, having many metaphoric meanings in various societies, is well used by the brewery as it was one of the first and the most enduring of American craft brewing. Sierra Nevada uses a graceful series of labels capturing the imagery of the Sierra Nevada landscape and ascertains the identity of the different products with color schemes rather than entirely new motifs. Both breweries represent excellence in both product and label quality, a correlation that is carried over to many of the other microbreweries throughout the land.

Perhaps no one better personifies the maverick attitude of the microbrewing industry than Bill Owens. Bill opened one of the first brewpubs in America, called "Buffalo Bill's Brewpub," and helped launch what was to be coined the "Microbrewing Renaissance," or "Revolution." An accomplished photo journalist, he would soon be able to add brewer, publisher and beer label designer to his resume. The labels of "Buffalo Bill's Brewpub" would contrast the refinement of Anchor and Sierra Nevada with humorous and audacious designs, a fact that demonstrates the flexibility of an enchanting and burgeoning industry.

"One day in the 1980s a friend of mine, a CPA, came into the brewpub bemoaning a recent divorce. As a CPA, he was acutely aware of the fact that he was going to lose his house, lose money, etc., etc... I suggested that we should make an 'Alimony Ale' to celebrate his divorce. I called a designer friend of mine, Karen Barry, told her the story, and she came up with a picture of Sweeney Todd from the Barber of Seville. On the original label a classified ad appeared featuring the CPA looking for a new woman, and included his phone number. The beer itself featured an unheard of amount of hops, which made it "The Bitterest Beer in America," which is formally trademarked and verified by the Siebel Institute.

"...A similar story is associated with the brewery's 'Pumpkin Ale.' The idea began when an assistant brewer was discussing how George Washington liked to make beer using various vegetables, including pumpkins. We brewed, using actual pumpkins, tasted it, then suddenly realized that the flavor that we love in pumpkin pie comes from all of the spices that you add. We ran across the street, got some pumpkin pie spices, put it in a coffee filter, and then added the pumpkin pie spice to the brew. The label design incorporates the pumpkin theme, but doesn't allude to the fact that the beer was inspired by George Washington."

Only in California!

ACME

CALIFORNIA

ANCHOR BREWING CO.

CALIFORNIA

ANCHOR BREWING CO.

CALIFORNIA

ANDERSON VALLEY

CALIFORNIA

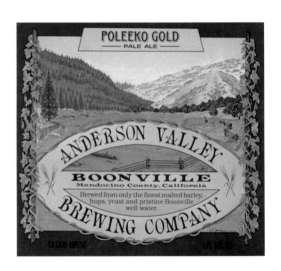

CALIFORNIA

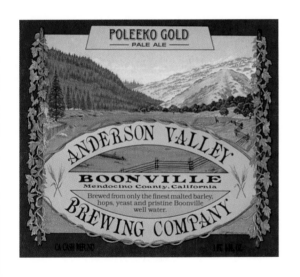

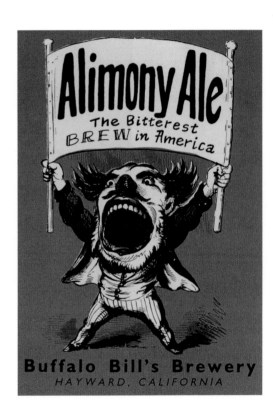

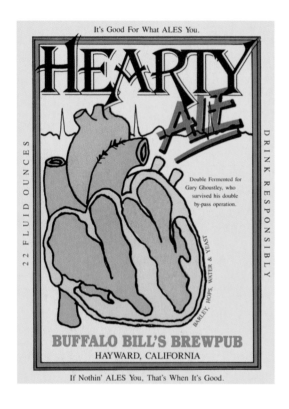

CALIFORNIA

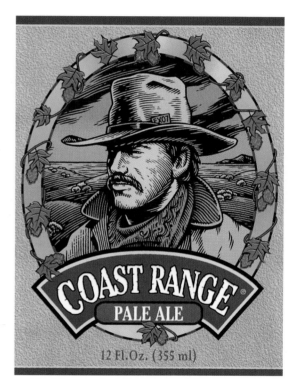

GOLDEN GATE

CALIFORNIA

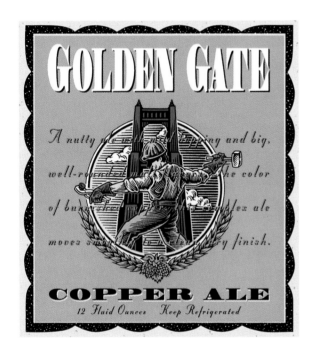

GORKY'S RUSSIAN

CALIFORNIA

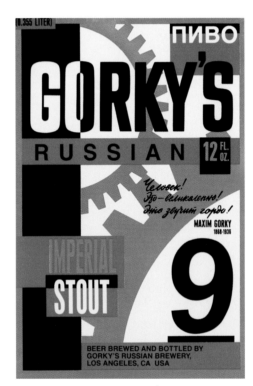

HECKLER BREWING CO.

CALIFORNIA

CALIFORNIA

CALIFORNIA

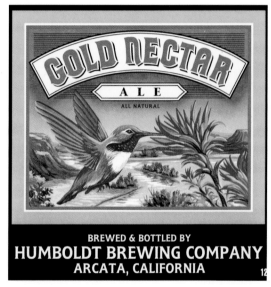

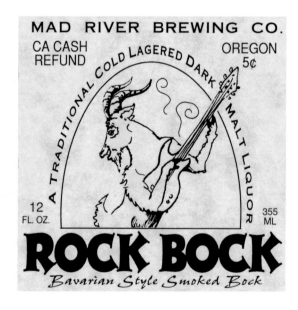

MAD RIVER BREWING CO.

CALIFORNIA

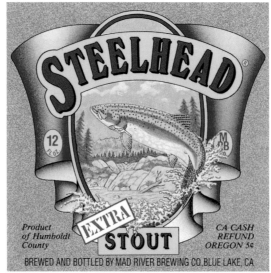

98

CALIFORNIA

CALIFORNIA

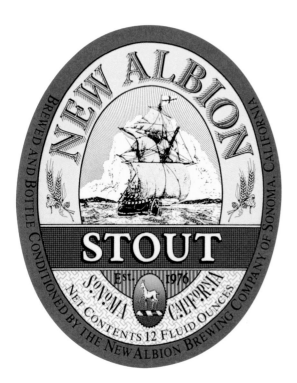

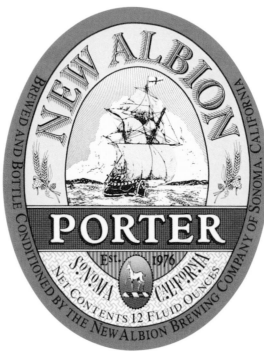

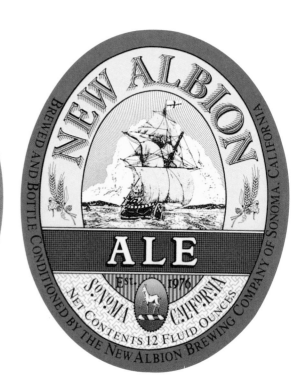

North Coast Brewing Co.

CALIFORNIA

Pete's Brewing Co.

CALIFORNIA

Santa Cruz Brewing Co.

CALIFORNIA

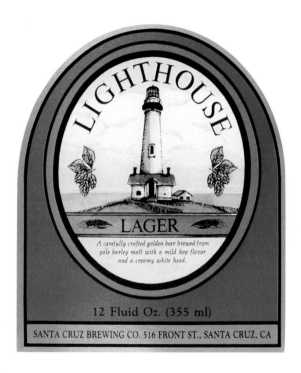

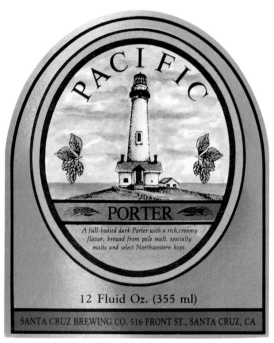

CALIFORNIA

SLO Brewing Co.

CALIFORNIA

St. Stan's Brewing Co.

CALIFORNIA

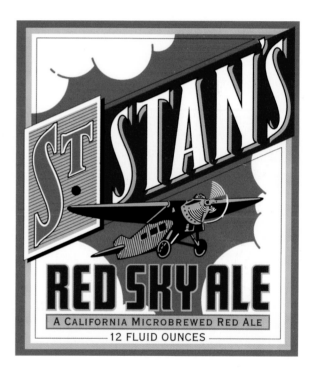

CANADA

There's a place where the wind blows cold and pure, where snow-covered mountains puncture the clouds, where sugar maples and oak woodlands linger lazily throughout the rugged countryside. No, it's not a beer commercial: the place is Canada. Home to moose and caribou, wolves and polar bears, Canada has become a metaphor for beer in advertising.

Beer commercial imagery aside, Canada is a unique country, vast and scarcely populated. The major cities exist only near the U.S. border, which exposes Canada's dependency on the U.S. economy. Even so, culturally Canada is a product of English and French influence. With the expeditions of Henry Hudson, Jacques Cartier, and Samuel de Champlain came the cultures of England and France, and the giants of brewing that would evolve into Molson and Labatt.

In recent years there has been a revolution in Canadian beer history, an affront to the standard of the giant breweries. Microbreweries and regional brewpubs thrived during the early '8os, and while the expanse of these smaller brewers has slowed, their popularity and success have given Canada a paradoxical beer personality. As the giant brewers continue to make the easy-drinking lagers and ales that are so tied in with beer-marketing culture, the regional breweries are rediscovering the traditional appeal of brewing with distinction.

The mass-market brands of Canada market their products using nationalistic pride. Whether it is in the packaging, on print ads, radio spots or television commercials, Canadian icons such as the maple leaf, hockey or a snow capped mountains will likely be involved. It is a charming representation of a country whose citizens are so proud of their heritage and is done in a more reserved and sophisticated manner than what a giant brewer in America would display. A possible explanation for this approach is the disadvantage that Canadian breweries have as compared to American owned and operated breweries. The high taxation that creates a wonderful health care system and excellent schools unfortunately creates a less-favorable economic environment. This fact is best demonstrated by the recent flight and troubles of several of Canada's beloved hockey franchises. Also, tricky inter-Province trade regulations and logistical transportation issues create serious obstacles that need to be dealt with tactfully. Therefore, perhaps, is the need for the giant breweries to embed an association of their products with Canada to diminish the possibility of "out-of-towners" coming in and setting up shop.

Smaller breweries in Canada are not encumbered by the global economic issues that the giant breweries deal with. Embracing the brewing cultures of their forefathers, Canada's craft brewers are producing a wide variety of classic beer styles. Dirk van Wyk, designer for the well-regarded Big Rock Brewery in Canada, aptly captures an artist's mentality of design for their craft breweries in the Great White North when asked about his philosophy of label creation:

"The process of design re-values... questioning with impossible questions/ answering with possible answers/ finding the bottom line below what you thought was the bottom line/ re-shaping boundaries of shape, colour, texture and meaning/ understanding the possible perceptions of the public/ coming to the edge of throwing it all away and starting again/ proportioning beyond mere measurement into the weighing of qualities and characteristics/ proportioning line to colour to shape to meaning and bringing it all to intention... Designing is an act of cultivation and control even it comes out looking perfectly natural-easy!"

The giant breweries of Canada have done their best to associate their products with the spirit and the icons of what is Canadian. However, the question arises—what is more "Canadian"— large scale corporate production or small-scale, craft products and artistic packaging?

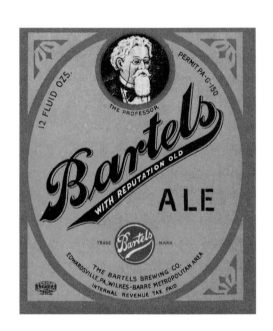

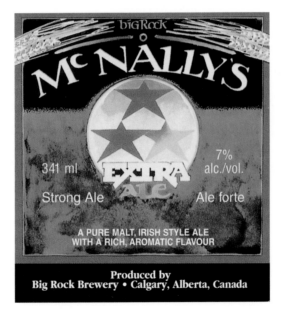

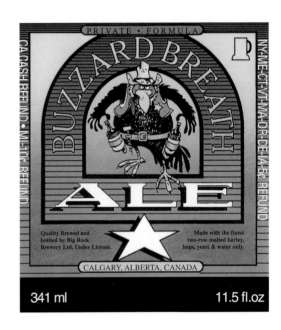

BIG ROCK BREWERY

CANADA

CANADA

CANADA

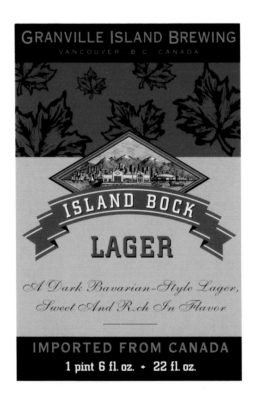

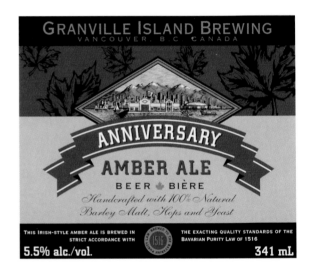

BRASSERIE MCAUSIAN

CANADA

THE WHISTLER BREWING COMPANY

CANADA

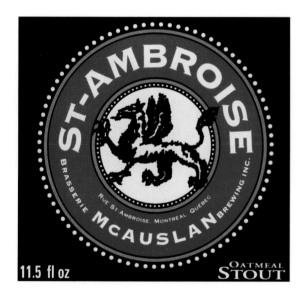

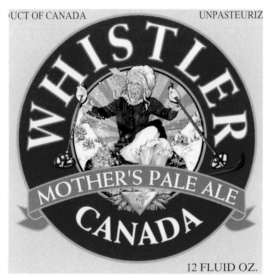

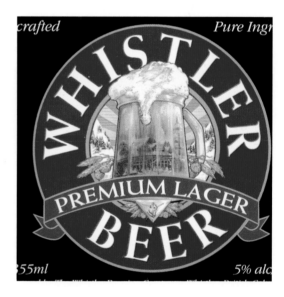

TREE BREWING CO.

CANADA

CANADA

UNIBROUE CHAMBLAY

CANADA

CANADA

EUROPE

Beer traces its beginnings to ancient Egypt and Mesopotamia. The practice of making beer most likely predates a more familiar use of grain—bread. The practice of brewing spread to Europe and, from the sack of Rome to the advent of the Renaissance, was made best in the Christian Abbeys. The Renaissance brought scientific pursuits back to Europe, and brewing techniques became more advanced. Probably the greatest advance took place by accident in the 15th century when Bavarian brewers stored, or "lagered" their beer in caves in the Alps. The cold brewing process produced a cleaner-tasting, clearer beer, today called "lager."

Brewing cultures have since developed in the Czechoslovakian Republic, Austria, Germany, Belgium, the U.K., Ireland, and in most other European nations. All of the great brewing cultures have developed distinctive products, drinking places, and, of course, packaging. The cultures of Europe led to variations on beer-making that reflect the personalities of the different regions—the subtle elegance of the Belgians, the disciplined harmony of the Germans, the melancholy poetry of the Irish—dispositions represented in their respective beer styles.

The Germans drink more beer per person than any other society on Earth. The immense amount of breweries produce classic German styles with changes in personality from region to region and with strong seasonal accents. Germany thus offers numerous beer varieties. Beer houses mark all of the countryside, though they are still more characteristic of the Bavarian South. These establishments always have a meticulously clean brewing area, and the brewer is often present. Unlike in the U.S. or Britain, where distinctions between microbreweries and brewpubs are obvious, in Germany drinking beer is so elemental that any establishment could very well brew. This is to the delight of any visiting beer lover. Formal brewing procedures and regulations are outlined, and are strictly followed. Beer labels, particularly the typography, reflect a traditional reverence for product and brewery.

The Belgian tradition of brewing is one of reverence, diversity, and elegance. Belgian beer styles are unique and differ greatly within the country. Beer is regarded as a more delicate beverage carefully chosen per occasion, tediously matched with different foods, and affectionately stored and served as if it were a fine vintage wine. The Belgian people are adverse to centralized institutions that the giant brewers represent. Belgium has been strong-armed, charged through, fought over, taken over, retaken over, and fighting for independence for long enough to appreciate the beauty of its unassuming diversity. The result is a culture of the most unique beer styles in the world. Belgian labels take much from wine but are, for the most part, as diverse as their beer products.

Lacking the sense of ceremony for meals like the Italians or the Spanish, the Irish, the British and the Scots more than make up for it with pub culture. The pub is the center of the beer culture in these lands, as patrons gather after Church or work to discuss matters of the day with their neighbors over a stout, a porter or a bitter. The pub could have very well been there before America was a country, and often it seems that the proprietor has been there just as long. Twenty years ago, Americans would be shocked at the difference between our mainstream products and that which you would be served up at one of these pubs, but the microbrewing revolution has brought the two much closer together. As our beer culture is just recently reemerging, the Irish, British and Scots have had their pub culture for centuries. Thus brand names are familiar and steeped in history, and are the focus of how beers are labeled.

Elsewhere in Europe, beer is widely consumed and marketed, with several giant brewers distributing to many of the countries. It is the emigrants of Europe's brewing nations who brought to America their brewing cultures and their particular characteristics which are reflected in America's many beer products. In the meantime, they have continued on with their centuries-old brewing culture, reflected in the products and incorporated into the labels.

AFFENPINSCHER

GERMANY

AYINGER

GERMANY

Brasserie Cantillion

BELGIUM

Brasserie d'Orval

BELGIUM

Brouwerij Lindemans

BELGIUM

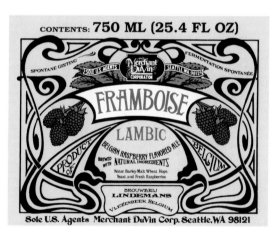

BROUWERIJ LINDEMANS

BELGIUM

CALEDONIAN BREWERY

SCOTLAND

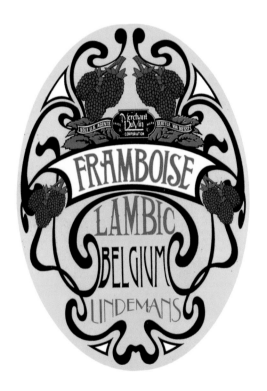

SCOTLAND

BELGIUM

INSELKAMMER

GERMANY

KAISERDOM-PRIVATBRAUEREI

GERMANY

KONIG LUDWIG

GERMANY

MELBOURN BROTHERS BREWERY

ENGLAND

MERRIMANS BREWERY

ENGLAND

MONT ST. GUIBERT

BELGIUM

MURPHY'S

IRELAND

N.V. BR. ALKEN-MAES

BELGIUM

ORKNEY BREWERY

England

PAULANER

Germany

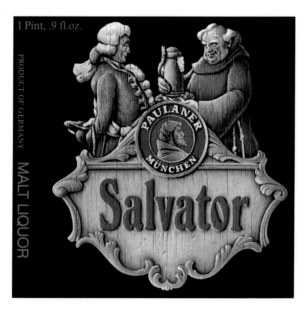

PAULANER

GERMANY

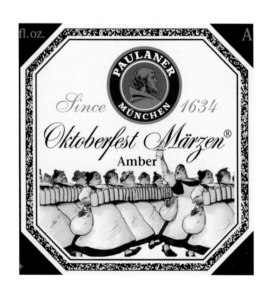

PINKUS MULLER BRAUEREI

GERMANY

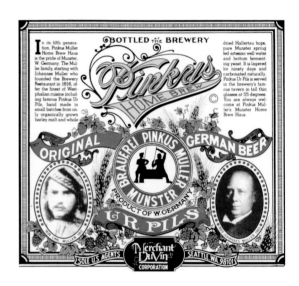

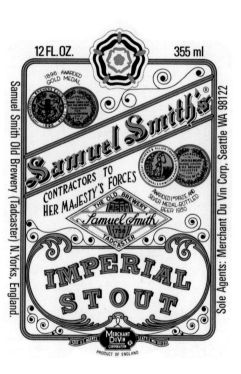

ENGLAND

WALES

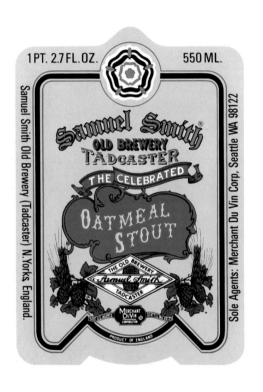

THE RAM BREWERY

ENGLAND

TIMMERMANS

BELGIUM

TRAQUAIR HOUSE

SCOTLAND

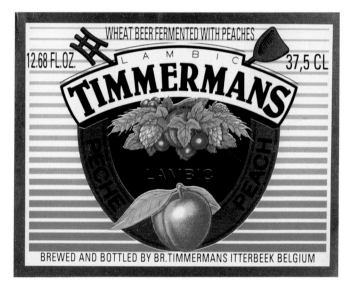

REST OF THE WORLD

The product that most of us refer to as "beer" developed primarily in Europe. As these European countries "explored" the world in hopes of expanding their respective empires, much of their cultures would be proliferated to far reaches of the world. European-style beers can be found on the Four Corners of the Earth—from China to South America, Australia to the Caribbean.

The art of beer making, or the creation of any fermented beverage for that matter, is inherent in almost every culture primitive to post-industrial. So it is not appropriate to state that the Europeans "gave" beer to the world, as most every non-European culture has in its customs the creation of a similar drink. That stated, what does make it into our economies are beer products that are at least somewhat familiar and generally, in style close to classic European beer types.

Occasionally, however, wonderful new products become available to the public. One example is the Brazilian Xingu Black Beer. Although created and imported by the American company, Amazon, Inc., the product is a wonderful collaboration of the indigenous peoples' and European settlers' traditions. The label of Xingu is actually taken from a map of the Amazon with a Txuchahamei warrior and a caiman.

"Down Under" in Australia and in neighboring countries, the European brewing culture is going strong. Beer consumption and export from the region is, and has been, very strong, as are most European-style products in the area. Most of the products are labeled reminiscent of their European ancestors, but the traditions are more loosely followed, allowing for an easy distinction when perusing a market's beer shelves.

Beer is a product that is produced nearly everywhere on earth. In America, it has just recently regained its rightful prominence and art status. The next chapter of the history of beer should deal with the success of products from other parts of the world—an excellent opportunity for a whole slew of unique packaging attributes, especially the label.

ARGENTINA

AUSTRALIA

SWAN BREWERY CO.

AUSTRALIA

TASMANIAN BREWERIES

TASMANIA

AMAZON, INC.

BRAZIL

BACKWORD

Sit back a moment and let your mind wander through your past. Try to remember your best first dates.

How did your date look—the details of the hair, the particular style of clothing, posture, eye color? Do you remember how little elements of the appearance built up suggestions in your mind about what to expect? Created a feeling, a mood?
Better yet, do you remember how self-consciously you went about creating the details of your own first impression?

Who said packaging wasn't important? If it isn't, why do we spend so much time on our own package? I don't think there's anyone who hasn't experienced the ability of a package to create a certain attitude, a certain predisposition towards a product. Walk the aisles of any supermarket and tell me packaging isn't working its butt off to connect your emotions to some product. And there is no doubt in my mind that beer does this best.

As the most democratic and populist of beverages, beer has a license to play, to experiment, to take risks. For many thousands of years we've been making and enjoying beer. It's the Everyman of beverages. Possibly the first advertisements were designed to attract consumers to one beer in preference to another.

Now with thousands of beers crowding the shelves and hundreds of new producers entering the industry, all bets are off these days on what passes for interesting packaging. And that's where today's visual excitement comes in. Not only are these new brewers trying out different classic beer styles, and pushing the limits of credulity in creating new styles, but they are also exploding the visual conventions of the industry.

No longer do nineteenth century type treatments, the almost stodgy embellished Germanic look, dominate beer labels. Today's brewery owner looks at these tiny billboards as a tabla rasa where they can make the ultimate positioning statement about their beer.

We have folk heroes and pet dogs, famous artists and famous writers, pastoral scenes and cityscapes, romantic moods and political statements, everything and anything under the sun. All to prepare you, get you in the mood, for the taste of their beer.

Yes, that little piece of paper, affixed to the outside of the bottle, symbolizes the heart and soul of the brewery, all of their wishes and dreams, as they deliver their beer—their ultimate art—to you.

So, sit down and enjoy the complexities and the sensory stimulation of a fine beer. Then turn to the label and see if it doesn't complement the beauty of the beer. Now, can you remember if that first date turned out as well?

Daniel Bradford
Publisher
All About Beer Magazine

P. S. Next time you cruise your beer shelves, imagining all the different flavors, think beauty pageant. See if that doesn't help your choice!